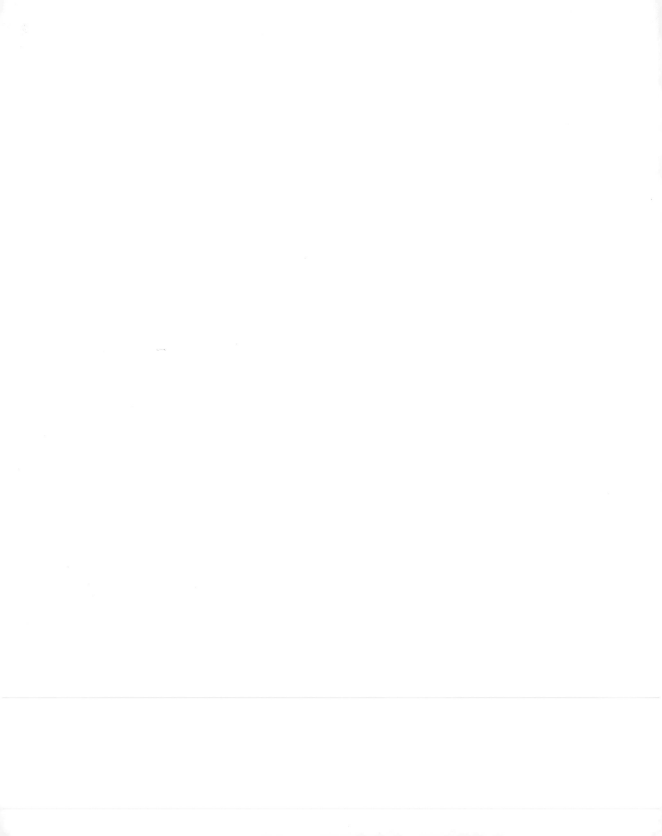

States

IOWA

by Angie Swanson

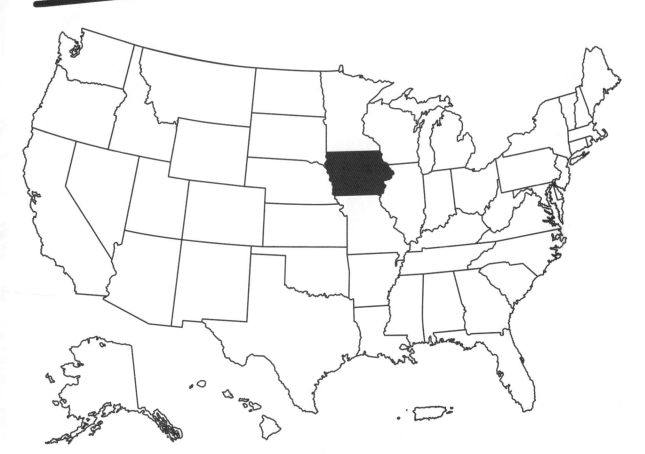

CAPSTONE PRESS
a capstone imprint

Next Page Books are published by Capstone Press,
1710 Roe Crest Drive, North Mankato, Minnesota 56003
www.mycapstone.com

Library of Congress Cataloging-in-Publication Data
Cataloging-in-publication information is on file with the Library of
Congress.
ISBN 978-1-5157-0402-7 (library binding)
ISBN 978-1-5157-0461-4 (paperback)
ISBN 978-1-5157-0513-0 (ebook PDF)

Editorial Credits
Jaclyn Jaycox, editor; Richard Korab and Katy LaVigne, designers;
Morgan Walters, media researcher; Laura Manthe, production specialist

Photo Credits
Capstone Press: Angi Gahler, map 4, 7; Corbis: CORBIS, 26, Michael S.
Lewis, 9; Dreamstime: Scott Griessel, 17; Getty Images: DEA PICTURE
LIBRARY, 12, Hulton Archive, top 19, Interim Archives, bottom 18;
Glow Images: Keystone Archives, top 18, Superstock, middle 19;
Library of Congress: Prints and Photographs Division Washington,
D.C., 28; Newscom: Album/Florilegius, 25; One Mile Up, Inc., flag, seal
23; Shutterstock: 3523studio, top 20, Alexander Davidyuk, top 24, amir
bajrich, bottom 20, brickrena, 15, Donna Beeler, middle 18, elinorb,
top 21, Henryk Sadura, 5, bottom left 8, HodagMedia, 6, Joseph Sohm,
16, MaxyM, cover, bottom right 8, Nancy Bauer, 7, Photographee.eu,
bottom 21, s_bukley, bottom 19, smereka, 14, bottom 24, Volt Collection,
13, Zack Frank, 10; SuperStock: Jim West/age fotostock, 11; Wikimedia:
British Library, 27, Josh deBerge, 29

All design elements by Shutterstock

Printed and bound in China.
0316/CA21600187
012016   009436F16

TABLE OF CONTENTS

Want to take your research further? Ask your librarian if your school subscribes to PebbleGo Next. If so, when you see this helpful symbol (↖) throughout the book, log onto www.pebblegonext.com for bonus downloads and information.

LOCATION

Iowa is a middle-sized state in America's Midwest region. Iowa is the only state whose east and west borders are formed by water. The Mississippi River creates Iowa's eastern border. The Missouri River forms its western edge. Iowa's north and south borders are perfectly straight lines. To the north is Minnesota. Missouri borders the south. Across the Missouri River to the west are South Dakota and Nebraska. Wisconsin and Illinois lie to the east, across the Mississippi. Des Moines, the state capital, is located near the center of the state on the Des Moines River. Iowa's biggest cities are Des Moines, Cedar Rapids, Davenport, and Sioux City.

PebbleGo Next Bonus!
To print and label
your own map, go to
www.pebblegonext.com
and search keywords:
IA MAP

Des Moines is home to more than 203,000 people.

GEOGRAPHY

Iowa's land is divided into three regions. These regions are the Dissected Till Plains, the Young Drift Plains, and the Driftless Area. The Dissected Till Plains lie mostly in southern Iowa. This area of rolling hills stretches to Iowa's northwest corner. The Young Drift Plains cover central and northern Iowa. This area has excellent farmland. Most of Iowa's natural lakes lie in this region. The Driftless Area runs along the Mississippi River on Iowa's northeast border. Iowa's highest point, Hawkeye Point, is near the Iowa-Minnesota border. It is 1,670 feet (509 meters) above sea level.

PebbleGo Next Bonus! To watch a video about Iowa's agriculture, go to www.pebblegonext.com and search keywords:

IA VIDEO

The Mississippi River creates Iowa's eastern border with Wisconsin.

Effigy Mounds National Monument overlooks the Mississippi River in eastern Iowa.

Legend

▲ Highest Point

◯ Lake

〜 River

Mississippi River

Turkey River

DRIFTLESS AREA

Wapsipinicon River

Cedar River

Iowa River

Spirit Lake

Hawkeye Point ▲

Okoboji Lakes

YOUNG DRIFT PLAINS

Big Sioux River

Floyd River

Little Sioux River

Missouri River

Boyer River

West Nishnabotna River

East Nishnabotna River

Nodaway River

DISSECTED TILL PLAINS

Raccoon River

Des Moines River

Red Rock Lake

Rathbun Reservoir

Thompson River

Chariton River

Mississi

Scale

Miles
0   20   40   60   80

0   20   40   60   80
Kilometers

N W E S

WEATHER

Iowa's climate can vary greatly. Iowa's average winter temperature is 19 degrees Fahrenheit (minus 7 degrees Celsius). The average summer temperature is 72°F (22°C).

Average High and Low Temperatures (Des Moines, IA)

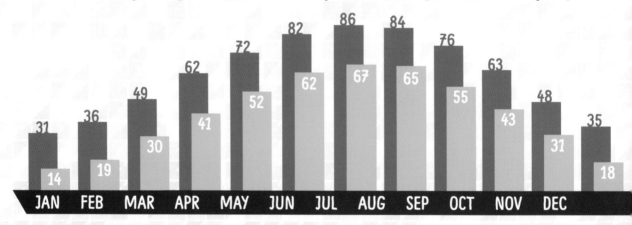

	JAN	FEB	MAR	APR	MAY	JUN	JUL	AUG	SEP	OCT	NOV	DEC
High	31	36	49	62	72	82	86	84	76	63	48	35
Low	14	19	30	41	52	62	67	65	55	43	31	18

Spirit Lake

Spirit Lake is a popular fishing destination and is also Iowa's largest natural lake. Spirit Lake is one of a chain of lakes in northwest Iowa near the Minnesota border.

Effigy Mounds

The Effigy Mounds National Monument includes more than 200 prehistoric mounds built by American Indians between 750 and 2,500 years ago. The mounds are shaped like animals, including birds and bears. The structures are located along the Mississippi River north of Marquette in northeast Iowa.

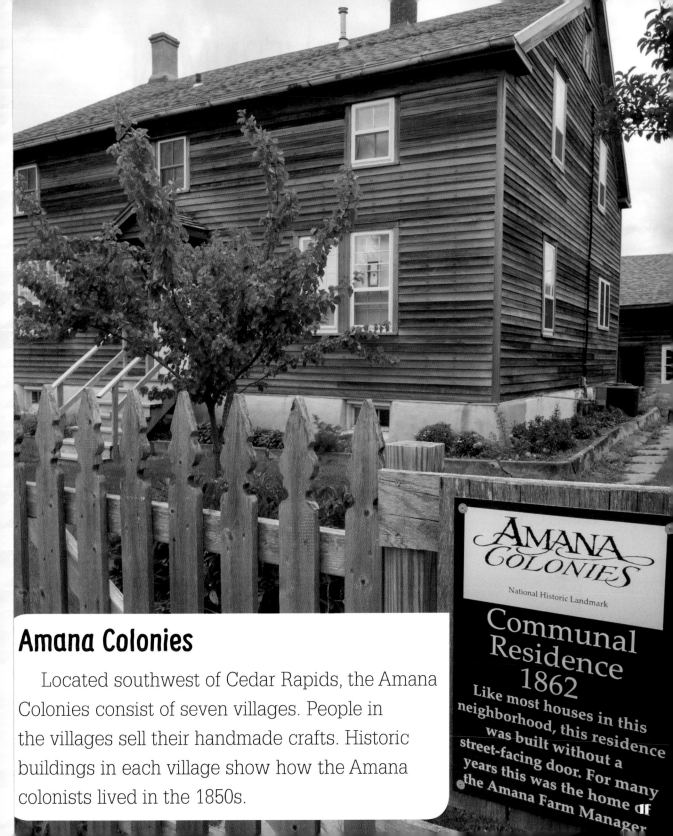

Amana Colonies

Located southwest of Cedar Rapids, the Amana Colonies consist of seven villages. People in the villages sell their handmade crafts. Historic buildings in each village show how the Amana colonists lived in the 1850s.

AMANA COLONIES

National Historic Landmark

Communal Residence 1862

Like most houses in this neighborhood, this residence was built without a street-facing door. For many years this was the home of the Amana Farm Manager

INDUSTRY

Iowa's economy is based on agriculture, manufacturing, and service industries. Farmland covers about 90 percent of Iowa. Iowa leads the United States in corn production, growing about 20 percent of the country's corn. Iowa is also a leading state in soybean production. Hogs are Iowa's top source of livestock income. Iowa raises about 25 percent of all hogs in the United States. Iowa also ranks among the top 10 states in raising beef and dairy cattle. Many of the state's manufacturing industries have close ties to agriculture.

Iowa has about 210,000 dairy cows.

These companies produce a wide variety of food products, including popcorn, bacon, oatmeal, and packed meats. Iowa's largest service industries are insurance, banking, and real estate. Tourism also contributes to service industry income.

Iowa leads the nation in percentage of land used for agriculture.

POPULATION

In the late 1800s, many Iowans came from Germany, Ireland, Great Britain, and other countries. They immigrated to the United States and settled in Iowa. Today most Iowans were born in the Hawkeye State. Iowa's citizens have a variety of backgrounds. Most Iowans have German, Scandinavian, Irish, or British heritage. Today about 90 percent of Iowa's population is white. African-Americans moved to Iowa after the Civil War (1861–1865). About 3 percent of the state's residents are African-Americans. Most Hispanic people came to Iowa from Mexico or Central America. Five percent of Iowans are Hispanic.

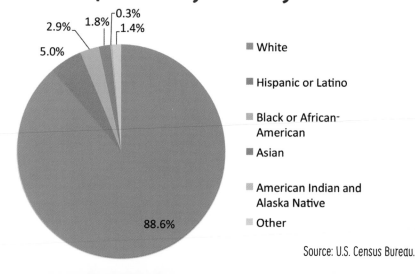

Population by Ethnicity

- 0.3%
- 1.4%
- 1.8%
- 2.9%
- 5.0%
- 88.6%

- White
- Hispanic or Latino
- Black or African-American
- Asian
- American Indian and Alaska Native
- Other

Source: U.S. Census Bureau.

About 2 percent of Iowa's population is Asian. Asian immigrants came from the Philippines, China, Japan, India, and Southeast Asia. American Indians make up less than 1 percent of Iowa's residents.

The Iowa State Fair is one of the largest in the country. It attracts more than 1 million people from around the world.

FAMOUS PEOPLE

Herbert Hoover (1874–1964) was the 31st U.S. president (1929–1933). He was born in West Branch and grew up in Oregon.

William "Buffalo Bill" Cody (1846–1917) was a frontier scout and expert marksman. He founded Buffalo Bill's Wild West Show, which toured the United States and Europe. He was born in Scott County.

Carrie Chapman Catt (1859–1947) played a leading role in the struggle to get women the right to vote. She also founded the League of Women Voters. She was born in Wisconsin and moved to Iowa as a child. She graduated from what is now Iowa State University.

Lee De Forest (1873–1961) was an inventor whose work led to the invention of the radio. He was born in Council Bluffs.

John Wayne (1907–1979) was an actor known for his tough cowboy roles. He appeared in more than 200 movies. He was born Marion Michael Morrison in Winterset.

Tom Arnold (1959–) is an actor, director, and comedian who has appeared in many movies. He was born in Ottumwa.

STATE SYMBOLS

Tree

oak

Flower

wild rose

Bird

eastern goldfinch

Rock

geode

PebbleGo Next Bonus! To make a dessert using an Iowa farming product, go to www.pebblegonext.com and search keywords:

IA RECIPE

MINING PRODUCTS

limestone, portland cement, sand and gravel, lime

MANUFACTURED GOODS

food products, machinery, chemicals, fabricated metal products, computer and electronic equipment, plastics and rubber products, furniture, paper

FARM PRODUCTS

corn, soybeans, milk, beef cattle, hogs

PROFESSIONAL SPORTS TEAMS

Iowa Barnstormers (AFL)

PebbleGo Next Bonus! To learn the lyrics to the state song, go to www.pebblegonext.com and search keywords:

IA SONG

IOWA TIMELINE

1600s — About 20 American Indian groups live in Iowa, including people of the Ioway, Sauk, and Mesquakie tribes.

1620 — The Pilgrims establish a colony in the New World in present-day Massachusetts.

1673 — French explorers Louis Jolliet and Father Jacques Marquette travel down the Mississippi River.

1682 — René-Robert Cavelier, also known as Sieur de La Salle, claims the Mississippi River Valley, including Iowa, for France.

1775–1783 American colonists fight for their independence from Great Britain in the Revolutionary War.

1788 French-Canadian adventurer Julien Dubuque becomes the first permanent European settler in Iowa.

1803 The United States buys a large area of land from France, including present-day Iowa. The sale was called the Louisiana Purchase.

1832 The U.S. Army defeats American Indians in the Black Hawk War, resulting in the American Indians being forced to move off a long strip of land along the Mississippi River in Iowa.

1838 Congress creates the Territory of Iowa.

1846

On December 28 Iowa becomes the 29th U.S. state.

1861–1865

The Union and the Confederacy fight the Civil War. Iowa fights for the Union.

1867

The first railroad across Iowa is completed from the Mississippi River to Council Bluffs.

1913

The Keokuk Dam opens in the southeast corner of Iowa. It generates electricity and improves transportation on the Mississippi River.

1914–1918 World War I is fought; the United States enters the war in 1917.

1920s Land prices rise and crop prices fall, causing an economic depression among Iowa's farmers.

1929 Iowa native Herbert Hoover becomes the 31st U.S. president.

1939–1945 World War II is fought; the United States enters the war in 1941.

1980s Iowa's economy suffers because of falling crop prices.

1985 Iowa establishes a lottery to raise money for the state.

1993 Major floods due to heavy rains cause more than $2 billion in damage to Iowa farms and property.

2010 The Lake Delhi Dam in eastern Iowa fails due to heavy rains and design issues, causing millions of dollars of damage to homes and businesses.

2015 The Iowa State Fair has record-breaking attendance. An estimated 1,117,000 people visited.

Glossary

agriculture *(AG-ruh-kul-chur)*—the science of growing crops

depression *(di-PRE-shuhn)*—a period during which business, jobs, and stock values stay low

economy *(i-KAH-nuh-mee)*—the ways in which a country handles its money and resources

ethnicity *(ETH-niss-ih-tee)*—a group of people who share the same physical features, beliefs, and backgrounds

executive *(ig-ZE-kyuh-tiv)*—the branch of government that makes sure laws are followed

frontier *(fruhn-TIHR)*—the far edge of a settled area, where few people live

immigrant *(IM-uh-gruhnt)*—someone who comes from abroad to live permanently in a country

industry *(IN-duh-stree)*—a business which produces a product or provides a service

legislature *(LEJ-iss-lay-chur)*—a group of elected officials who have the power to make or change laws for a country or state

limestone *(LIME-stohn)*—a hard rock used in building; made from the remains of ancient sea creatures

prehistoric *(pree-hi-STOR-ik)*—from a time before history was recorded

Read More

Ganeri, Anita. *United States of America: A Benjamin Blog and His Inquisitive Dog Guide.* Country Guides. Chicago: Heinemann Raintree, 2015.

King, David. *Iowa.* It's My State! New York: Cavendish Square Publishing, 2014.

Marciniak, Kristin. *What's Great About Iowa?* Our Great States. Minneapolis: Lerner Publications, 2015.

Internet Sites

FactHound offers a safe, fun way to find Internet sites related to this book. All of the sites on FactHound have been researched by our staff.

Here's all you do:

Visit *www.facthound.com*

Type in this code: 9781515704027

Check out projects, games and lots more at
www.capstonekids.com

Critical Thinking Using the Common Core

1. What does the blue bar on Iowa's state flag stand for? (Key Ideas and Details)

2. Iowa is called "The Hawkeye State." What are some other nicknames that you think would be appropriate for Iowa? Use the text to support your answer. (Integration of Knowledge and Ideas)

3. The Effigy Mounds created by the American Indians are considered prehistoric. What does prehistoric mean? Use the glossary for help with your answer. (Craft and Structure)

Index